JOHN & JACQUELINE KENNEDY

PRESIDENTS
and
FIRST LADIES

iBooks
Habent Sua Fata Libelli

Ruth Ashby

Please visit our web site at:
www.ibooksforyoungreaders.com
Manhanset House
POB 342
Dering Harbor, New York 11965

Library of Congress Cataloging-in-Publication Data
Ashby, Ruth.
John & Jacqueline Kennedy / by Ruth Ashby.
p. cm — (Presidents and first ladies)
Includes bibliographical references and index.

1. Kennedy, John F. (John Fitzgerald), 1917-1963—Juvenile literature. 2. Onassis, Jacqueline Kennedy, 1929—1994—Juvenile literature. 3. Presidents—United States—Biography—Juvenile literature. 4. Presidents' spouses—United States—Biography—Juvenile literature. I. Title.
E842.Z9A84 2004   973.922'092—dc22   [B]   2004047960

ISBN: 978-1-59687-661-3

Copyright © 2005 by Byron Preiss Visual Publications
Produced by Byron Preiss Visual Publications Inc.
Project Editor: Kelly Smith
Photo Researcher: Bill White

Photo Credits: AP/Wide World: 15, 22, 23, 40, 41, 42; HistoryPictures.com: 4 (top and bottom), 5, 6, 7, 8, 9, 10, 12 (top and bottom), 13 (top and bottom), 16, 18, 19, 20, 21, 24 (bottom), 28, 29, 35, 36, 37, 38, 39; John Fitzgerald Kennedy Library: 11, 24 (top), 25, 26, 27, 31, 32, 33, 34

All rights reserved. No part of this book may be reproduced, stored in a retrieval system, or transmitted in any form or by any means, electronic, mechanical, photocopying, recording, or otherwise, without the prior written permission of the copyright holder.

August 2024

CONTENTS

Introduction 4

Chapter One   **Jack** 5

Chapter Two   **Jackie** 12

Chapter Three   **Onto the World Stage** 16

Chapter Four   **New Frontiers** 22

Chapter Five   **Foreign Matters** 27

Chapter Six   **Hail and Farewell** 31

Chapter Seven   **The Legend** 39

Time Line 43

Glossary 44

Further Information 45

Index 47

About the Author 48

Words that appear in the glossary are printed in **boldface** type the first time they occur in the text.

INTRODUCTION

On May 31, 1961, President and Mrs. John F. Kennedy stepped off Air Force One onto the Paris runway and into the hearts of the French people. "*Vive Jacqui!*" the waiting crowd chanted. "Long live Jackie!" During the state visit, Jack Kennedy impressed French president Charles de Gaulle with his intelligence and knowledge of international affairs. However, it was his wife who overwhelmed the old general with her beauty, culture, and love of French history.

At a luncheon that afternoon, Jack famously said, "I do not think it altogether inappropriate to introduce myself to this audience. I am the man who accompanied Jacqueline Kennedy to Paris."

John Fitzgerald Kennedy, thirty-fifth president of the United States, in an official White House portrait.

Jacqueline Bouvier Kennedy, first lady of the United States, in 1961.

Jack and Jackie Kennedy, the most glamorous president and first lady ever to live in the White House, were a charismatic couple and a superb political team. To many people in the 1960s, they seemed as dazzling as the prince and princess in a fairy tale. Revelations about the Kennedys' private life have since led us to realize that the fairy tale was an illusion, yet their imperfections highlight their very real virtues: courage, grace, intelligence, and a capacity to grow. Four decades later, Jack and Jackie Kennedy continue to fascinate us.

CHAPTER ONE

JACK

The two-story gray house in the Boston suburb of Brookline, Massachusetts, was in an uproar. Upstairs, in the master bedroom, the second son of Joseph Patrick and Rose Fitzgerald Kennedy was being born. Afterward, Rose made a neat entry on an index card:

*John Fitzgerald Kennedy
born Brookline, Mass. (83 Beals Street) May 29, 1917*

At the birth of John's elder brother, Joe Jr., two years before, his proud grandfather had announced, "He is going to be president of the United States." No one made such grandiose predictions for this most recent addition. Someone should have.

John Fitzgerald Kennedy, nicknamed Jack, was the newest member of an extremely ambitious family. From the time in the 1840s and 1850s when their Irish ancestors first stepped onto the shores of America to escape the potato famine, the Kennedys and the Fitzgeralds had relentlessly pursued money and power. Jack's grandfather on his mother's side, John Francis Fitzgerald—known as Honey Fitz—was a popular congressman and mayor of Boston. From Honey Fitz, Jack inherited not only his name but oodles of irrepressible Irish charm. Jack's father's father, Patrick J. Kennedy, was a saloonkeeper who made a fortune as a whiskey importer before going into state politics. Fiercely competitive, he told his son Joseph, "Always come first. Second place is failure."

Rose Kennedy poses with her first five children, c. 1922. From left to right: Rose, Eunice, Kathleen, Rosemary (sitting), John, and Joseph Jr.

On the Brink

In the late 1930s, Europe teetered on the edge of a precipice. Under Nazi chancellor Adolf Hitler, Germany was building up its military. So was Italy, under **totalitarian** leader Benito Mussolini. In 1936, Hitler and Mussolini created an alliance called the Rome–Berlin Axis. Both leaders wanted to expand their nations' territories. Italy seized Ethiopia in 1935. Germany rolled into Austria in 1938. Anxious to avoid war, the French and British met with the Germans in Munich, Germany, on September 29, 1938. Hitler promised to halt his aggression. Elated, Prime Minister Neville Chamberlain of Great Britain declared that he had ensured "peace in our time," but six months later, Hitler seized Czechoslovakia—and then invaded Poland. World War II had begun.

Joe Kennedy learned the lesson well. He pushed himself to achieve—at age twenty-five, he became the youngest bank president in Boston. In a few years, he would fulfill his boyhood vow to make a million dollars by the time he was thirty-five. In the 1920s and 1930s, he consolidated and extended his wealth by investing in the stock market, the movie industry, and the liquor trade. No matter how large his fortune, however, he discovered that as an Irish Catholic in Boston, he could not scale the heights of old-money Protestant society. His sons, he decided, would do it for him.

Joe raised his children to be champions, too. There would be seven more children after Jack: Rosemary, Kathleen, Eunice, Patricia, Robert (Bobby), Jean, and Edward (Ted). In this rough-and-tumble household, success was the only guarantee of love—or even attention. The children grew up with their father's slogan ringing in their ears: "We want no losers here, only winners!" In the ongoing family Olympics—in swimming, sailing, golf, baseball, and football—skinny Jack was no match for his bigger and tougher older brother. Joe Jr., the heir apparent, was the focus of his parents' hopes for national fame.

Constant illness put Jack at a disadvantage. Whooping cough, measles, chicken pox, flu, colds, allergies—he had them all. He almost perished at age three from scarlet fever and at age fourteen from appendicitis. "We used to laugh about the great risk a mosquito took in biting Jack Kennedy," his

Jack (center, front row) and his seventh-grade classmates at the Riverdale Country Day School in the Bronx, c. 1929. In 1927, the Kennedy family moved to New York, where Joseph Kennedy had established a new business.

brother Bobby said later. "With some of his blood, the mosquito was almost sure to die."

Being sickly did have its compensations. For one thing, when Jack was ill, his mother paid him more attention than usual. Rose Kennedy was a brisk, cold woman not given to displays of affection. "My mother never hugged me," Jack once complained to his best friend, Lem Billings. "Never!"

Lying in bed also gave Jack lots of time to read. He was a voracious reader, gobbling up tales of romance, chivalry, and adventure, such as the legends of King Arthur and the novels of Sir Walter Scott. As he grew older, he turned to history and biography.

A World-class Education

At age fourteen, he was off to Choate, a boarding school in Connecticut. "Ratface," as Jack was called because of his thin face, was still too slight to become a sports star, so he became a rebel instead. His room was a mess, his study habits slipshod, and his punctuality nonexistent. Yet his wit and good humor won everybody over. Even his much-provoked headmaster declared, "I never saw a boy with as many fine qualities as Jack has that didn't come out right."

In his first two years at Harvard, Jack rarely cracked a book, preferring to concentrate on swimming and social clubs. One classmate remembered him as a "gangling young man with a slightly snub nose and a lot of flap in his reddish-brown hair."

The summer after Jack's freshman year, he and Lem Billings set off on a grand European tour. While they explored castles and art museums, Jack began to focus on foreign affairs. Europe in 1937 was in a state of suspense. Germany and Italy, both governed by **fascist dictatorships**, threatened neighboring countries. One urgent question preyed on everybody's mind: Would there be another European war? Fascinated, Jack

Christmas card, 1935. Choate classmates Ralph "Rip" Horton, Lemoyne "Lem" Billings, and Jack "Ken" would remain lifelong friends.

A fascinated Jack reads the latest news from Europe, Sept. 22, 1939.

discussed the situation with everyone he met—farmers, bankers, and soldiers.

When President Franklin D. Roosevelt appointed Joe Kennedy ambassador to Great Britain at the end of the year, Jack took the opportunity to learn more about the world of **diplomacy.** At Harvard, he started to take his course work more seriously and brought his grade point average up from a gentleman's C to a B+, at which point he was eligible to write an honors thesis in political science. He decided to concentrate on contemporary affairs.

Adolf Hitler invaded Poland on September 1, 1939, and the world changed. Two days later, Jack, Joe Jr., Kathleen, and their parents watched from the Strangers' Gallery (gallery for visitors) in the House of Commons as Great Britain declared war on Germany. Jack then had a topic for his thesis: Why had England failed to prepare for war? He wrote it eagerly, engrossed in the subject. Jack graduated cum laude, or with praise or distinction. His thesis earned a magna cum laude, or with great honors.

He showed his thesis to one of his father's friends, *New York Times* columnist Arthur Krock, who said, "It would make a very welcome and very useful book." Revised and published, *Why England Slept* became a best-seller. At age twenty-three, Jack Kennedy had his first taste of fame.

The Young Hero

The United States remained neutral—but it seemed only a matter of time before it joined the war. Jack felt his place was in the military, yet because of his continuing health problems, he failed the physical exams for both the U.S. Army and the U.S. Navy. For years, he had been in and out of hospitals for chronic diseases of the colon and stomach. In addition, he had back pain that seemed to grow steadily worse. The usual explanation was that it came from an old football injury, but it seems likely that the condition was aggravated by the steroid medication he took for his intestinal problems.

Despite constant pain, Jack was desperate to serve, so Joe Kennedy pulled some strings, and in October 1941, Jack became an ensign in the Navy, assigned to a desk job in Washington, D.C. He was there when the Japanese attacked **Pearl Harbor** on December 7.

Jack applied for sea duty and was accepted to naval officer training school. A year later, Jack was made a lieutenant and assigned to the South Pacific as commander of an 80-foot (24-meter) patrol-torpedo boat, the *PT-109*. It was one of a group of PTs ordered to attack a Japanese **convoy** on August 1, 1943. The combat operation was a disaster. In the dark, moonless night, the *PT-109* crew couldn't see the menacing shape of a Japanese destroyer bearing down on them. "So this is how it feels to die!" Jack thought as the destroyer collided with his boat.

Of the thirteen-member crew, two men were killed instantly. Kennedy and five others pulled themselves up on a floating remnant of the hull. Voices floated over the oily, debris-strewn water. When Jack swam out to investigate, he found five members of his crew. Patrick McMahon's face and hands were severely burned, so Jack gave his life jacket to the injured Charles Harris and towed McMahon himself.

Nine hours later, still no rescuers had arrived. The survivors decided to swim to the nearest island, several miles away. For five hours, Jack towed McMahon by holding the straps of his life jacket in his mouth. The tiny island held no food and no water, so Jack pushed the exhausted crew to swim to the larger Olasana Island, where at least there were some coconut trees.

On the sixth day, two Melanesian islanders found the crew. Jack carved a message into a coconut shell: NATIVE KNOWS POSIT HE CAN PILOT 11 ALIVE NEED SMALL BOAT KENNEDY. The Melanesians carried the message to a New Zealand military camp.

World War II

World War II pitted the Allied powers—the United States, Great Britain, France, the **Soviet Union**, China, and others—against the Axis powers—Germany, Italy, Japan, and others. It was fought on three major fronts: Europe, North Africa, and the Pacific. Over a period of six years, 1939–45, the conflict caused the deaths of approximately 60 million people—soldiers and civilians—across the globe. It was the deadliest and most destructive war in human history.

The coconut shell on which Jack scratched a rescue message. Years later, Kennedy would keep the shell, preserved in plastic as shown here, on his desk at the White House.

Lieutenant John F. Kennedy enjoying himself at the elegant Stork Club in New York City, 1944.

A few days later, the crew of the *PT-109* was rescued.

The news of the rescue blazed across the country. "Kennedy's son saves 10 in Pacific," the *Boston Globe* announced. Jack was a hero.

Of course, Jack was pleased that he had proved himself under fire, but he was modest about his exploits. When someone asked how he had become a hero, he said wryly, "It was easy. They cut my PT boat in half." He was awarded the Purple Heart and the Navy and Marine Corps Medal.

Jack's older brother was not so fortunate. After joining the navy and serving as a bomber pilot in World War II, Joe Jr. died when his plane exploded over England at the start of a risky mission in August 1944. Jack had a renewed sense of the fragility of life.

A Step into Politics

The burden of Jack's father's expectations fell on the second son. "It's your responsibility to go into politics," Joe Kennedy told Jack point-blank. In 1946, Jack decided to run for Congress from a congressional district in Boston. Soon politics had him hooked. It was exciting, it was challenging, it was important. Above all, Jack admitted, "The fascination about politics is that it's so competitive."

He plunged into the campaign. By seven o'clock on most mornings, Jack was down on the Charleston docks, shaking hands with the workers. All day he pounded the pavement, knocking on doors and visiting firehouses, barbershops, and taverns. In the evenings, he spoke at one of the women's tea parties organized by his sisters. The whole Kennedy family pitched in to get their brother elected. His father spent an unprecedented amount of money—$300,000—buying his son publicity.

In the end, the voters decided they liked the skinny young man with the modest manner and dazzling grin. Jack Kennedy won the Democratic nomination and then, in this heavily Democratic district, the general election. On January 3, 1947, he was sworn in as a United States congressman.

The Kennedy clan in Hyannis Port, c. 1948. From left to right: Jack, Jean, Rose, Joseph, Patricia, Robert, Eunice, and Edward (front).

Jack Kennedy's congressional career was unremarkable. As a freshman congressman, he had little power to initiate **legislation** or make a difference, and he didn't try terribly hard to do either.

It didn't help that his first two years in office were difficult personally. While visiting his sister Kathleen in London in 1947, he was diagnosed with Addison's disease, an illness that gradually destroys the adrenal glands, which are small hormone-producing organs on top of the kidneys that affect the body's metabolism and immune system. "That American friend of yours," his doctor told one of Jack's English friends, "he hasn't got a year to live." Luckily for Jack, though, the new miracle drug cortisone was effective against Addison's. He was dependent on it for the rest of his life.

A year later, Kathleen, the sibling to whom he was closest, died in a tragic plane crash. Jack was devastated. "How can there possibly be any purpose in her death?" he asked a friend in anguish. The loss, together with his chronic illness, made him very aware of his own mortality. "The point is," he said to an old friend, "that you've got to live every day like it's your last day on earth. That's what I'm doing."

As far as Jack was concerned, living life to the fullest didn't mean lingering in the **House of Representatives.** Jack was on the fast track to fame and power. Next stop: the **Senate.**

CHAPTER TWO

JACKIE

Janet Bouvier with Jack "Black Jack" Bouvier (right) at a horse show, 1931.

Born on July 28, 1929, to a wealthy family in Southampton, New York, Jacqueline Lee Bouvier enjoyed a childhood of ease and privilege. Her mother, Janet, was a proper, stylish society matron with a will of iron. Her father, Jack, was a charming playboy with a perpetual tan. That and his jet-black hair earned him the nickname Black Jack. Little Jackie inherited her father's broad face, with its wide-set eyes and straight dark eyebrows, but she owed her intelligence and strong will to her mother.

Even when very young, Jackie demonstrated the composure that became her trademark. Once, while playing in Central Park with her nanny and younger sister, Lee, Jackie strayed off. When she realized she was alone, Jackie walked up to a policeman and announced, "My nurse and sister seem to be lost!"

Like her mother, Jackie became a superb horsewoman. From the moment she began riding at age two, she showed courage and stamina. Her mother advised her, "Never fall off a horse, but if you do, get up and get right back on again." Jackie also evinced an early flair for fashion, wearing riding outfits that looked like miniature versions of her mother's.

Family Troubles

What seemed to outsiders like the perfect family was split by discord, however. Jackie's beloved father was losing money on the stock market, and the family was

At age five, Jackie already displayed her characteristic grace and poise. Here, she rides with her mother at the East Hampton horse show on Long Island.

12

living well above its means. Janet and Black Jack had violent disputes about money and his flamboyant infidelities. When voices were raised and china shattered, Jackie would take Lee by the hand and escape into another room.

Her troubled home life turned Jackie into a rebel. Very bright and studious, she was known as a good student at Chapin, the private girl's school she attended in New York City's Upper East Side, but now she became a troublemaker. Her third-grade teacher remembered that Jackie was "very clever and very artistic and full of the devil."

Jackie became a regular at the office of Miss Stringfellow, the headmistress. One day, Miss Stringfellow figured out a way to get through to her. "I know you love horses and that you yourself are very much like a thoroughbred," she told the young equestrienne. "You can run and you have staying power. You're well built and you have brains. But if you're not properly trained, you'll be good for nothing." Like a high-spirited racehorse, Jackie would have to learn discipline—or she'd never make it out of the starting gate.

Jackie often withdrew into the world of books, reading works such as Margaret Mitchell's *Gone with the Wind* and Daphne du Maurier's *Rebecca*. For hours on end, she read, sketched, and wrote poetry. When she was ten, she gave her father a poem, illustrated with a sketch of herself on the beach, black hair streaming in the wind. She wrote:

> *I can think of nothing I want more*
> *Than to live by the booming blue sea*
> *As the seagulls flutter around me.*

She signed it, "Me—1939."

Jack and Janet finally bowed to the inevitable and obtained

The young equestrienne at age eleven, with her favorite horse, Danseuse.

Ten-year-old Jackie with her dog, Tammy.

a divorce in June 1940. In 1942, Janet remarried a man with impeccable social credentials and enormous wealth, Hugh D. Auchincloss II. As a result, Jackie and Lee inherited a whole new family of step siblings and, eventually, half brothers and sisters.

In Love with Learning and Life

During her teenage years, Jackie continued her love affair with art and literature at Miss Porter's in Connecticut. A natural linguist, Jackie learned Italian and Spanish as well as French. At graduation, she received an award for excellence in literature. When asked to list her ambitions in the class yearbook, she was forthright: "Not to be a housewife."

At age eighteen, Jackie made her formal debut into society. At 5 feet 7 and a half inches (171.5 centimeters) tall, with long legs and a radiant smile, she had a natural sense of elegance. An enthusiastic society columnist anointed her the debutante of the year. Jacqueline Bouvier, he gushed, "[is] a regal brunette who has classic features and the daintiness of Dresden porcelain. She has poise, is soft-spoken and intelligent, everything the leading debutante should be." An old friend remembered, "Young men were constantly trying every kind of trick to make her go out with them," but Jackie had no steady boyfriend.

Jackie continued her French studies her first two years at Vassar College in New York and was delighted to go to Paris for a junior year abroad. When she came back, Jackie transferred to George Washington University in Washington, D.C., which boasted an excellent French department, but she longed to return to Paris. She was delighted to learn about a contest sponsored by *Vogue* magazine. The winner of the Prix de Paris would spend six months as a junior editor in Paris before transferring to New York. She decided to apply.

Asked for a self-portrait, Jackie wrote that she had "a square face and eyes so unfortunately far apart that it takes three weeks to have a pair of glasses made with a bridge wide enough to fit over my nose." She described her intellectual growth, pointing out that

Jackie poses with a press camera while working for the *Washington Times-Herald*.

during her first trip abroad, "I learned not to be ashamed of a real hunger for knowledge, something I had always tried to hide, and I came home . . . with a love for Europe that I am afraid will never leave me."

The editors at *Vogue* were impressed by the amusing and original young woman and offered her the coveted prize, but her mother made her turn the offer down. If Jackie went off to Europe, Janet thought, she might never come back.

Instead, after graduation, Jackie got a job at a local newspaper, the *Washington Times-Herald*. As "inquiring camera-girl," she interviewed and photographed a variety of people on topics of the day. She pleased Janet by becoming engaged to a rich, socially prominent young businessman named John G. W. Husted, Jr. It looked as if Jackie would fulfill all her mother's dreams by becoming Mrs. Husted and settling down to a life of quiet privilege.

It was at this point that she met a certain dashing young congressman from Massachusetts.

CHAPTER THREE
ONTO THE WORLD STAGE

No warning bells went off the first time Jacqueline Bouvier met John F. Kennedy at a dinner party in 1951. She was already engaged; he was busy running for the U.S. Senate. The timing was wrong. A year later, Jackie had broken her engagement. When she ran into Jack at another party, she "knew instantly that he would have a profound, perhaps disturbing, influence on her life."

Jack and Jackie Kennedy on their wedding day, September 12, 1953.

A Matched Pair

John Kennedy was known as Washington's most eligible bachelor. Tall and perpetually tan, with blue eyes and a thick mop of hair, he had a magnetic effect on everyone who met him. As an old girlfriend said, Jack "had the charm that makes birds come out of their trees." Women threw themselves at him, and he loved it. Yet he knew that, someday soon, he would have to get married. A bachelor could be elected senator—but never president. Besides, Jack enjoyed children and wanted to have a family.

From the beginning, he was intrigued by Jackie. They shared much in common: a love of reading, a longing for the sea, a wry wit, a sense of the absurd. They both devoured biographies, English literature, history. They both had had troubled childhoods, with difficult mothers and philandering fathers. Jackie was touched by Jack's story of the "little boy, sick so much of the time, reading history, reading the Knights of the Round Table . . ." Gradually, Jackie fell deeply in love. For his part, Jack, though more emotionally distant, found that here was someone he could genuinely love.

Jackie was much more introspective than Jack and not very interested in the gritty day-to-day events of practical politics. She would choose a good book any time over the turmoil of a political rally or the exhausting schedule of a campaign.

Theirs was an unusual courtship. Jack was constantly on the road, campaigning for the Senate. He would call her "from some oyster bar," she remembered later, "with a great clinking of coins, to ask me out to the movies the following Wednesday in Washington. . . . He was not the candy-and-flowers type, so every now and then he gave me a book." She went to the Kennedy summer home in Hyannis Port, on Cape Cod, Massachusetts, to meet his energetic family. "Just watching them wore me out," she said. Like Jack, she loved swimming and sailing, but the family's endless touch football games were too intense.

In November 1952, Jack won his election. Finally, he had more time to pay attention to Jackie. The next May, when Jackie went to London to cover the coronation of Queen Elizabeth II for the *Times-Herald*, he wired her a telegram: ARTICLES EXCELLENT, BUT YOU ARE MISSED. LOVE, JACK. When she returned, he was waiting with a diamond-and-emerald engagement ring.

Becoming a Family

Their wedding on September 12, 1953, was the society event of the year. A crowd gathered outside St. Mary's Church in Newport,

The newlyweds with members of their wedding party.

Rhode Island, to ogle the handsome couple. Jackie looked radiant in an ivory taffeta dress and her grandmother's lace veil. The veil hid a secret sorrow— Jackie had just found out that her father, nervous before the wedding, had been drinking in his hotel room, so she went down the aisle on the arm of her dignified stepfather, Hugh Auchincloss II.

Jackie had found her prince—but not her happy ending. The first year of marriage was difficult for both of them. Engrossed in work and unwilling to give up his bachelor freedom, Jack was rarely around. Even worse was his persistent philandering. Her experience of her father had led Jackie to expect a certain amount of infidelity from a husband, but it still hurt. Then, to make matters worse, she had a miscarriage.

For his part, Jack was plagued by increasingly severe back pain. A year after the marriage, he was on crutches most of the time. His doctor told him that without surgery, he would end up in a wheelchair. Unfortunately, his Addison's disease made him especially prone to infection. If he opted for an operation, he was told, he had a 50 percent chance of dying. For Jack Kennedy, life in a wheelchair was a fate worse than death. He decided to take the gamble.

On October 10, 1954, Jack underwent back surgery. Three days later, he went into a coma. The family stood by, terrified, as a priest administered the last rites, but Jack hung in there—and finally beat the odds. When the first operation was not a success, he had another one four months later.

While he was recovering, Jack began to work on a project he had been thinking about for a while. It was a book about eight senators who had risked their careers—and sometimes their lives—to defend causes they believed in. Still flat on his back, Jack needed a lot of help. Jackie and Ted Sorensen, his legislative aide, did most of the research. The three of them worked on the book together, with Jack and Ted writing and rewriting, and Jackie taking dictation and typing. Titled *Profiles in Courage,* the final book won the 1957 Pulitzer Prize for biography. Jack dedicated it to "my wife, Jacqueline, whose help during all the days of my convalescence I cannot ever adequately acknowledge."

Jack's illness had brought them together. Then, a year later, came the answer to their dreams. A daughter, Caroline Bouvier Kennedy, was born on November 27, 1957. It was, Jackie said, "the very happiest day of my life." Caroline turned the Kennedys into a real family.

In 1958, Jack ran for a second Senate term and won by a landslide. It was just the start, however. Now, he told Jackie, he was going to run for president. Republican Dwight D. Eisenhower, a popular president, would be leaving office in 1960. Jack didn't dare wait another four—or eight—years to make his bid. Given his history of health problems, he knew that might be too late. He had to seize the moment—1960 was his year.

The Race for President

Jack was a unique presidential candidate in some ways. For one thing, at forty-three years old, he was the youngest man ever to run for the office. He knew that his youth and good looks were two of his greatest assets. Despite his continued health problems, he projected an image of vigor (or "vigah," as Kennedy would say in his strong Boston accent).

Also, if Kennedy won, he would be the first Catholic president. Many people worried that this meant he would have to take orders from the pope. Jack assured them that he believed strongly in the separation of church and state. "Judge me on the basis of my record of fourteen years in Congress," he told a group of Protestant ministers. "I do not speak for my church on public matters—and the church does not speak for me."

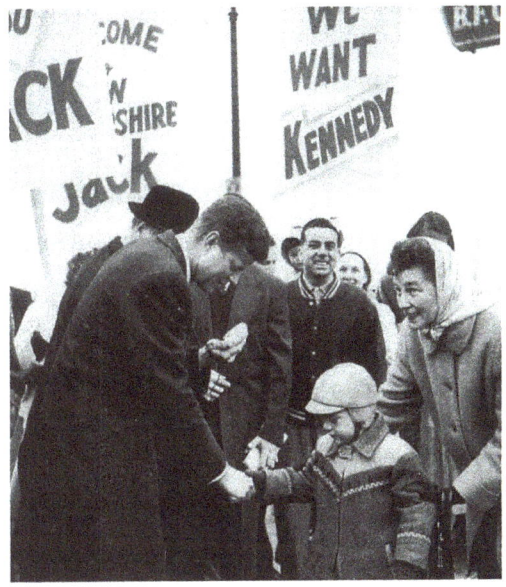

Kennedy greets a young supporter in New Hampshire during his run for the Democratic presidential nomination, February 1, 1960.

Kennedy campaigning in West Virginia, May 1960. He promised voters in this poor, coal-mining state that, if elected, he would do what he could to alleviate poverty.

First, Jack had to prove his appeal to the whole country, not just to New England. In his private plane, the *Caroline,* he crisscrossed the nation. With the rest of the Kennedys, he braved Wisconsin in winter. He went to West Virginia and witnessed real poverty for the first time. He went to Maryland, Indiana, and Oregon. "I married a whirlwind," Jackie said wryly. "He's indestructible. People who try to keep up with him drop like flies, including me."

She did her best, though, at least at the start of the campaign. To Italian audiences in Boston's North End, she spoke Italian; in Cajun Louisiana, she spoke French; in Wisconsin, she ventured a few words in Polish. People across the country were enchanted by her glamour and shy, gracious manner.

Jack appreciated her effort. "I just can't believe it," Jack said after his wife had spent an hour talking to striking railroad workers in West Virginia. "I'm so proud of Jackie." She kept up the effort until late spring, when she dropped out of the campaign after learning she was pregnant again. Their son, John F. Kennedy, Jr., would be born on November 25, soon after the national election.

At the convention on July 14, Kennedy wrapped up the Democratic nomination for president. Afterward, his main rival, Texas senator Lyndon B. Johnson, sent Kennedy a message. "LBJ," Johnson wrote, "now means 'Let's Back Jack.'" Kennedy took the hint. His first act was to tap Johnson for vice president. As a Texan, Johnson would help balance the ticket and win over voters in the South.

Kennedy's nomination acceptance speech sounded the keynote of his campaign: new leadership for a new era. "It is a time . . . for a new generation of leadership," he declared. "New men to cope with the new problems and new opportunities. . . . We stand today on the edge of a new frontier, the frontier of the 1960s—a frontier of unknown opportunities and perils—a frontier of unfulfilled hopes and threats."

Kennedy's Republican opponent would be Richard Nixon, a seasoned politician who was Eisenhower's vice president. In foreign affairs, Kennedy and Nixon both positioned themselves as strong on defense and tough on **communism.**

On domestic issues, their differences were more obvious, especially in the area of **civil rights.** On October 16, activist Martin Luther King, Jr., was jailed for protesting the **segregation** of an Atlanta department store. His wife, Coretta Scott King, was worried that if he went to jail his life would be in danger. At the urging of Jackie and others, Jack gave Coretta King a phone call, asking her to let him know if he could be of help. It was a small gesture, but it demonstrated Kennedy's growing support for civil rights.

Jack and Jackie greet enthusiastic supporters in a ticker tape parade in New York City on October 19, 1960, just one month before the election. Nearly eight months pregnant, Jackie spoke Spanish to voters in Spanish Harlem and Italian in Little Italy.

The highlight of the race was four televised debates between the candidates. The TV screen showed Kennedy at his best: self-confident and authoritative in his dark suit. Nixon, by contrast, looked sweaty and defensive. Afterward, most commentators agreed that Kennedy had "won" the debates.

As voting results began to come in on the evening of November 8, 1960, Jack, Jackie, and the rest of the Kennedy clan watched and waited in Hyannis Port. By 3:00 A.M., the race was still too close to call.

At 8:30 that morning, Caroline ran into her father's bedroom. "Good morning, Mr. President," she greeted him gleefully.

Kennedy had indeed won the election—by only 118,555 of 68,837,000 votes cast. He had won 303 of 537 **electoral college** votes. It was the smallest margin of victory since 1888. Later that morning, a tired but jubilant Jack Kennedy acknowledged his victory and thanked his supporters. "So now," he told the assembled reporters, "my wife and I prepare for a new administration—and a new baby."

CHAPTER FOUR: NEW FRONTIERS

On January 20, 1961, President John F. Kennedy was sworn into office before an audience of 20,000 shivering Washington spectators and millions of TV viewers. Despite the bitter cold, Jack was bareheaded and coatless. He had spent months working on his **inaugural address,** gathering suggestions from his staff, revising and polishing it. The final draft—short, lucid, and eloquent—had the lofty inspirational tone for which he was striving. It ended with a clarion call to selfless patriotism:

"And so, my fellow Americans," Kennedy declared, "ask not what your country can do for you—ask what you can do for your country."

As Jack turned away from the podium, Jackie murmured, "Oh, Jack, you were wonderful." Across the nation, Americans were moved and impressed. Even Eisenhower had to admit that the speech was "fine, very fine." Today, Kennedy's inaugural address is recognized as one of the best in American history.

John F. Kennedy at his **inauguration**, January 20, 1961.

An Inspiring Start

John F. Kennedy would be president for only two years, ten months, and two days. The promise of his life would be unfulfilled, his work remain forever undone, yet his "thousand days" in office left an indelible memory.

One of his first acts as president was to enlist thousands of young people inspired by his vision of national service. In March 1961, Kennedy established the Peace Corps, an organization devoted to sending Americans overseas to help out in needy countries. He hoped Peace Corps volunteers would be goodwill ambassadors for the United States, embodying American ideals through action.

In those first months, he also seized the initiative on space flight. In April, the nation was surprised and disturbed when Soviet cosmonaut Yuri Gagarin became the first human to go into space *and* to orbit Earth. A month later, American astronaut Alan Shepard went up in a short **suborbital** voyage. Jack and Jackie watched the fifteen-minute flight together in the Oval Office. The space race was on.

Shepard's success revived American self-confidence. Kennedy took advantage of the triumph to reaffirm the nation's commitment to space exploration. On May 25, 1961, he told Congress, "I believe that this nation should commit itself to achieving the goal, before this decade is out, of landing a man on the Moon and returning him safely to Earth." The audience exploded in cheers. Eight years later, his dream came true.

American Royalty

The Kennedys took the nation by storm. Their grace, style, and elegance made them the closest thing to royalty the country had seen since George and Martha Washington. They were models for everything, from fashion to sports. A new generation of American men went bareheaded in imitation of Jack, who hated hats. The new Kennedy fitness program had children doing sit-ups and running the 50-yard (46-meter) dash.

As for Jackie, she inspired a rage for sunglasses, pillbox hats, and simple, sleeveless dresses. An editor of *Women's Wear Daily* wrote, "As a consumer, as distinguished from a designer, Jackie has been the greatest influence [on fashion] of any woman of her time."

Jackie's pet project, though, was the White House. When she moved in, she told a friend, the executive mansion looked like "a hotel that had been decorated by a wholesale furniture store during

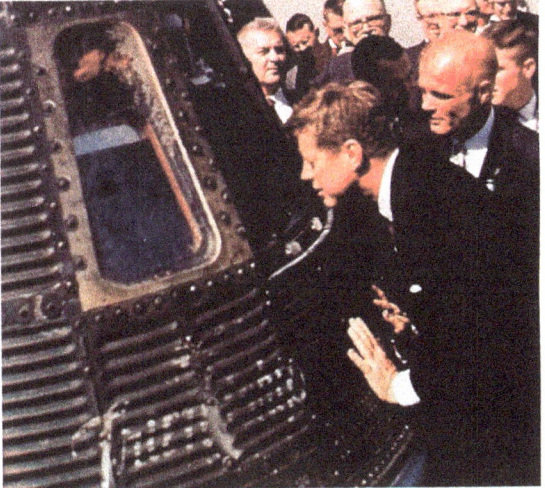

With astronaut John Glenn by his side, President Kennedy inspects space capsule *Friendship 7*. On February 20, 1962, Glenn became the first American to orbit the Earth. He came back to a hero's welcome.

President and Mrs. Kennedy watch the America's Cup sailboat race on September 15, 1962, from the deck of the USS *Joseph P. Kennedy, Jr.*, named after the president's older brother. Jackie looked as elegant on shipboard as she did in the reception rooms of the White House.

a January clearance." To turn it into the "first house in the land," she pored through dozens of books on White House history and interior design. Her goal was not redecoration, she insisted, but restoration, and that was a "question of scholarship."

After making a thorough search of White House storage rooms and private collections, she brought back Thomas Jefferson's inkwell, George Washington's armchair, and Abraham Lincoln's china. When she was done, Jackie gave the American people a televised tour of the refurbished executive mansion. "The White House is as it should be," she concluded. "It's all I ever dreamed for it."

"The first house in the land," Jackie thought, "should play host not only to foreign dignitaries and national leaders but also to poets, scientists, and artists." At Jacqueline Kennedy's state dinners, some of the world's greatest musicians and artists were invited to entertain. Once, the Kennedys hosted a dinner for all living Nobel Prize winners. Glancing around at the distinguished company, Jack quipped, "I think this is the most extraordinary collection of talent, of human knowledge, that has ever gathered at the White House, with the possible exception of when Thomas Jefferson dined alone."

With its composer and musical director, the Kennedys discuss an orchestral score commissioned for the inaugural concert. As first lady, Jackie made the White House a showcase for the arts.

Conscientious in her public duties, Jackie was also concerned about her privacy. Two days after the election, she told a reporter, "I feel as though I have just turned into a piece of public property. It's frightening to lose your anonymity at thirty-one." She mastered what friends called the PBO—the polite brush-off—for members of the press or public she found too inquisitive. Once, when a journalist asked her what the family's new German shepherd puppy ate, she smiled and replied, "Reporters."

She didn't guard just her own privacy. She wanted her children, Caroline and John Jr., to have as normal an upbringing as possible. She created a nursery school on the third floor, where they could play with friends their own age. The children had a playground, complete with a tree house, swing set, and trampoline.

In her busy schedule, Jackie made sure that she had enough time for her children. "If you bungle being a mother," she once said, "nothing else you do well matters very much."

Jack, too, was a proud and affectionate parent. "Aren't they great?" he would say to people when he showed them the pictures in his wallet. Caroline and John Jr. often ran into his room in the

Jackie Kennedy shares a tender moment with John Jr. in the White House nursery. John Jr. was born November 25, 1960.

John F. Kennedy's Inaugural Address

John Kennedy's idealistic inaugural address inspired young people across America, as he had hoped it would. Here is an excerpt:

"Let the word go forth from this time and place, to friend and foe alike, that the torch has been passed to a new generation of Americans—born in this century, tempered by war, disciplined by a hard and bitter peace, proud of our ancient heritage—and unwilling to witness or permit the slow undoing of those human rights to which this nation has always been committed, and to which we are committed today at home and around the world.

Let every nation know, whether it wishes us well or ill, that we shall pay any price, bear any burden, meet any hardship, support any friend, oppose any foe to assure the survival and the success of liberty.

This we pledge—and more. . . .

And so, my fellow Americans, ask not what your country can do for you—ask what you can do for your country.

My fellow citizens of the world: ask not what America will do for you, but what together we can do for the freedom of man."

mornings, as Jack, still in bed, was speed-reading through a dozen newspapers. If he heard them playing on the lawn outside the Oval Office, he would clap his hands so they could dart in and get some candy. The public loved the candid pictures of Caroline dancing on the office rug and "John-John" peering out from beneath the president's desk. Time with his children offered a brief respite from the pressures of the president's life.

A delighted Kennedy watches Caroline and John Jr. dancing in the Oval Office, October 10, 1962.

CHAPTER FIVE

FOREIGN MATTERS

Assuming the presidency was a jolt for Jack Kennedy. "In eleven weeks, I went from senator to president, and in that short space of time, I inherited Laos, Cuba, Berlin, the nuclear threat, and all the rest," he said. In the early 1960s, the United States was in the middle of the **Cold War** with the Soviet Union, or the Union of Soviet Socialist Republics (U.S.S.R.), and the rest of the Eastern European Communist bloc. The Soviet Union had dangerous nuclear power, and the United States felt vulnerable as never before.

Kennedy signing the order to **blockade** Cuba during the Cuban Missile Crisis, October 23, 1962. He was president during the tensest days of the Cold War.

Containing Communism

Communism had gained a foothold in the Western Hemisphere in 1959, when revolutionary Fidel Castro seized control of Cuba. By the time Kennedy was inaugurated, there were already military and Central Intelligence Agency (CIA) plans under way to topple Castro from power. Jack was told that with U.S. assistance, Cuban exiles would invade the island. Other Cubans would spontaneously rise up to join the exiles.

Kennedy gave the go-ahead. On April 17, 1961, U.S. boats landed 1,500 exiles at Cuba's **Bay of Pigs.** Instead of a popular uprising, the invaders were greeted by 20,000 well-armed Cuban troops. Most of the exiles surrendered and the invasion collapsed in disaster. When the **Joint Chiefs of Staff** urged Kennedy to send in U.S. troops, he refused. American troops would not be involved directly.

"How could I have been so stupid?" Kennedy scolded himself. He knew that erroneous CIA information and a gung-ho military were basically at fault, but he blamed no one but himself. His press statement said, "President Kennedy has stated from the beginning that as president he bears sole responsibility." Privately, though, he vowed never again "to rely on the experts" completely. Instead, he would depend on his own knowledge and common sense. It was a lesson that would stand him in good stead in the coming years.

Relations between the Communist Soviet Union and the democratic United States soon deteriorated. That August, the Soviet-controlled East German government began to build a wall through the middle of Berlin. After World War II, Berlin was split down the middle into West Berlin, controlled by the United States, Great Britain, and France; and East Berlin, controlled by the Soviet Union. When more and more East Berliners crossed to the West, the Communists decided to stem the flow by erecting a barrier. In a show of support for West Berlin, Kennedy sent in 1,600 U.S. troops to secure the area. However, tensions between East and West continued and the wall remained until 1989.

President Kennedy and Secretary of State Dean Rusk in discussion. A fellow cold warrior, Rusk worked with Kennedy to contain Communism.

Thirteen Days in October

The greatest crisis of Kennedy's presidency began on October 15, 1962. While Jack was still in bed, his national security advisor, McGeorge Bundy, delivered the bad news. Aerial photographs taken by U2 spy planes had revealed that the Soviets were installing nuclear missiles in Cuba, just 90 miles (145 kilometers) from the coast of Florida. It was the greatest threat to national security since World War II.

Kennedy immediately summoned a group of advisors to assess the situation. Over the next thirteen days, the Executive Committee of the National Security Council—known as ExComm—hashed out plans and counterplans to eliminate the nuclear threat.

★ FOREIGN MATTERS

The Kennedy brothers, from left to right: Robert (Bobby), Edward, and John. Bobby, Jack's attorney general, would become senator from New York in 1964. In 1968 he was assassinated while campaigning for the Democratic nomination for president. Ted followed in Jack's footsteps and won election as a senator from Massachusetts in 1962.

The military suggested an immediate aerial attack to take out the missiles. At first, Kennedy was inclined to agree, but he knew that any kind of attack might trigger a Russian retaliation—and spark an all-out nuclear war. Such a war, Kennedy felt, would be the "final human failure."

Secretary of Defense Robert McNamara had another idea—a naval blockade to prevent Soviet weapons from entering Cuba. Over the next few days, ExComm debated the options. More and more, Kennedy disliked the idea of the air strikes, which would kill thousands of Cubans and risk setting the Soviets on a path to destruction. A blockade, on the other hand, would give Soviet premier Nikita Khrushchev a chance to back off and save face.

On October 20, Kennedy called Jackie at their country house in Virginia and asked her to return to Washington with the children. "We are very, very close to war," he explained. A few days later, he suggested she move to a secret underground shelter outside Washington. However, she refused to leave him alone in the White House.

On October 22, Kennedy gave a speech on national television to 100 million Americans, at that time the largest television

The Cold War

After World War II, the world settled into an ongoing state of tension between communist and non-communist countries called the Cold War. In 1944 and 1945, the Allies had defeated the Germans by trapping them between three armies. American, British, and other Allied forces advanced from the west and south. The Soviets advanced from the east. The armies met in Germany, splitting the nation into American-, British-, French- and Soviet-controlled zones. After the war, the U.S.S.R. continued to occupy the nations of Eastern Europe, including East Germany, and made them part of the Communist bloc. The U.S., British, and French zones became West Germany. In 1946, British statesman Winston Churchill warned that an "iron curtain has descended across the continent."

For the next forty-five years, the United States tried to contain communism around the world. This policy led to involvement in two wars, the **Korean War** and the **Vietnam War.** It also led to an arms race, as each nation tried to establish superiority in both nuclear and conventional weapons. Not until 1991, with the breakup of the U.S.S.R., did the Cold War end.

---

audience ever. He announced the blockade and warned, "All ships of any kind bound for Cuba will, if found to contain cargoes of offensive weapons, be turned back." Across the United States, the tension mounted.

By October 24, 1962, the blockade of 180 American aircraft carriers and destroyers was in place. Military readiness increased to Defense Condition 2, just below a state of war. Soviet ships were speeding toward the blockade line.

In the Cabinet Room, ExComm awaited developments. Jack and and his brother Bobby, now attorney general, stared at each other across the table, imagining the unimaginable. Bobby wrote later, "Was the world on the brink of a holocaust and had we done something wrong?"

An aide handed a message to John McCone, the director of the CIA. "Mr. President," McCone announced, "we've just received information that all six Soviet ships currently identified in Cuban waters . . . have either stopped or reversed course."

Everyone breathed a sigh of relief. "We're eyeball to eyeball," Secretary of State Dean Rusk said, "and I think the other fellow just blinked."

The crisis wasn't over yet. It took many days of negotiations before Khrushchev agreed to remove the missiles from Cuba in "the cause of peace," but the most dangerous moment had passed.

Kennedy had averted violence and, possibly, a nuclear war. It was his finest hour.

CHAPTER SIX

HAIL AND FAREWELL

By the spring of 1963, well into the second year of his presidency, Jack Kennedy was clearly enjoying himself. Historian Arthur Schlesinger remembered that Kennedy "loved being president, and at times he could hardly remember that he had ever been anything else." When a reporter asked Kennedy how the job was going, he quipped, "I have a nice home, the office is close by, and the pay is good." The American public was enamored of him and of Jackie, who was expecting another child that summer.

Shaping a Legacy

Of course, Kennedy was beset by nagging problems at home and abroad—civil rights, poverty, communism, Vietnam, Cuba, the ever-present possibility of a nuclear war. "Every president," he wrote that year, "must endure a gap between what he would like and what is possible."

In order to narrow that gap, Kennedy tried to improve relations between the United States and the Soviet Union by establishing a private "hot line" between the White House and the **Kremlin.** In June, Kennedy signaled a change in U.S.–Soviet relations in a graduation address at American University. "Let us re-examine our attitude toward the U.S.S.R.," he said. "In the final analysis, our most basic common link is that we all inhabit this small planet. We all breathe the same air.

President Kennedy giving a commencement speech at American University, June 10, 1963. In his address, he talked about his hopes for world peace and a new era of improved communications with the Soviet Union.

31

On June 26, 1963, Kennedy mounted a platform overlooking the concrete and barbed-wire wall that divided East from West Berlin. Appalled by the sight, he addressed a crowd of cheering West Berliners.

We all cherish our children. And we are all mortal." He announced that the United States was ending its testing of nuclear weapons and asked the Soviet Union to follow suit.

By July 26, 1963, the U.S., the U.S.S.R., and Great Britain had agreed on a test ban treaty, the first arms-control agreement of the Cold War. Nuclear testing in the atmosphere, in the ocean, and in space would cease. Kennedy regarded the treaty as his most important achievement to date, "a shaft of light [that has] cut into the darkness."

He also visited Berlin that June and addressed a million people at the Berlin Wall. There was a "sea of human faces," Ted Sorensen remembered later, chanting "Kenne-dy, Kenne-dy." Kennedy, shocked by the concrete wall topped by barbed wire, delivered one of his most rousing speeches. Berliners, he told the cheering crowd, were a heroic barrier against communism. "All free men, wherever they may be, are citizens of Berlin, and therefore, as a free man, I take pride in the words, '*Ich bin ein Berliner*'" (by which he meant, "I am a citizen of Berlin").

Her pregnancy prevented Jackie from traveling to Europe. On August 7, Jackie was rushed to Otis Air Force hospital with labor pains. Little Patrick Bouvier Kennedy, born prematurely, weighed only about 4 pounds 10 ounces (2 kilograms). For two days, he struggled for breath. Jack was at the baby's bedside when he died at 4 A.M. on August 9. "He was such a beautiful baby," the president told an aide. "He put up quite a fight." Then, Jack broke down and sobbed.

Patrick's death brought Jack and Jackie together as never before. Despite their public image as the perfect couple, Jack's infidelities had not ended when he entered the White House, and their relationship was sometimes strained. Now, friends noted, he was especially tender toward his grieving wife. They spent most of the next month together with their children. Jackie was sure that their relationship had reached a turning point.

At the end of August, the capital witnessed one of the most inspiring events of Kennedy's presidency: the March on Washington. Kennedy's civil rights record was uneven. Although he believed it was time for the United States to guarantee equal rights for its African-American citizens, he dragged his heels. Congress, he knew, was not ready to pass the necessary laws. Many southern Democrats—who Kennedy might need to win the 1964 election—were diehard segregationists. Nonetheless, years of civil rights demonstrations had finally convinced him that it was time to make a stand. In June, he proposed a major new civil rights law, the most far-reaching since **Reconstruction**.

Jack, John Jr., Jackie, Caroline, and some favorite dogs on vacation at the Kennedy family compound in Hyannis Port, Massachusetts, August 14, 1963. Just a week before, they had lost a son, Patrick Bouvier Kennedy.

When he heard about the proposed march, Kennedy initially opposed it. He was afraid it would harm his chances of getting the bill passed, but when he saw that the march would definitely proceed, he and Bobby tried to make sure it would go smoothly.

On August 28, 1963, more than 250,000 black and white Americans marched peacefully up the National Mall and assembled in front of the Lincoln Memorial in Washington, D.C. The last speaker on the program, Dr. Martin Luther King, Jr., delivered an electrifying speech. "I have a dream," King declared, "that my four little children will one day live in a nation where they will not be judged by the color of their skin, but by the content of their character." That evening, at a White House reception, a newly inspired Kennedy clasped King's hand and repeated simply, "I have a dream."

The president meeting with the leaders of the March on Washington, August 28, 1963. Dr. Martin Luther King, Jr., is third from the left.

That fall, Kennedy and his advisors were especially concerned about the situation in South Vietnam, a small Southeast Asian country engaged in a civil war with Communist-controlled North Vietnam. For nearly ten years, the U.S. government had supported South Vietnam in an effort to stave off victory by the North. Like many others, Kennedy believed that if South Vietnam fell to the Communists, the rest of Southeast Asia would follow, like a row of dominoes. As a result, he had increased the number of U.S. military "advisors" in Vietnam to 16,000.

Kennedy saw the United States as increasingly bogged down in an unstable country with weak leadership. On November 2, 1963, the South Vietnamese president, Ngo Dinh Diem, was assassinated in a **coup** carried out by Vietnamese generals. Although the United States had not directly planned the coup, it had known about it ahead of time and not prevented it. Privately, Kennedy doubted that the new military government had sufficient popular support to survive, either. On the morning of November 21, Kennedy asked the State Department "to organize an in-depth study of every option we've got in Vietnam, including how to get out of there."

Then, he and Jackie left for Texas.

Tragedy in Dallas

Texas was one of the first stops in Kennedy's campaign for the 1964 presidential election. He was very pleased when Jackie agreed to come along with him, not just because he enjoyed her company but because she was so popular with voters.

The next morning, when he stepped outside his Fort Worth hotel, the waiting crowd shouted, "Where's Jackie?"

Jack gestured toward the hotel. "Mrs. Kennedy is organizing herself," he said, grinning. "It takes her a little longer, but of course, she looks better than we do when she does it."

That day, Friday, November 22, they were on their way to Dallas, where the Kennedys would drive in a motorcade through the streets of the city. There had been some dispute about going to Dallas, known to be an ultraconservative city with many Kennedy haters. On the plane, Jack showed his wife an anti-Kennedy ad from the *Dallas Morning News*. "We're heading out into nut country today," he said. "But, Jackie, if somebody wants to shoot me from a window with a rifle, nobody can stop it, so why worry about it?"

"It was a terribly hot day," Jackie remembered afterward, "just blinding all of us." She and the president were sitting in the rear seat of a limousine convertible, with Texas governor John Connally and his wife in the front seat. As the car neared an overpass, it slowed down a bit.

Jack and Jackie Kennedy waving to the Dallas crowds a few seconds before Jack was shot. Texas governor John Connally, also wounded by the sniper's bullets, and his wife are in the front seat of the limousine.

From the Texas School Book Depository on a nearby hill, a lone gunman thrust a rifle out the sixth-floor window and fired three shots at the president.

The second bullet hit the back of Jack's neck and tore out through his throat and then into Connally's back, hand, and thigh.

Lyndon B. Johnson takes the oath of president of the United States on the presidential airplane Air Force One just an hour and a half after the assassination. A stunned Jackie stands beside him, her clothes stained with her husband's blood.

Connally would later recover from his wounds. Kennedy's left hand flew up to his neck, but he did not fall forward because the brace he wore for chronic back pain kept him erect.

Seconds later, another bullet crashed into the back of his head and out the right side. In that instant, Jack Kennedy was no more.

Jackie shouted, "Oh, God, they have shot my husband!" In shock, she tried to climb out on the trunk of the car, but she was saved by a Secret Service agent who shoved her back into the seat and clambered in beside her.

"My God, they've killed Jack," Jackie moaned, "they've killed my husband." As the limousine sped toward the nearest hospital, Jackie bent over his body. "Oh, Jack. Oh Jack, I love you."

At 1:00 P.M. central time, doctors at Parkland Hospital told her what she already knew—the president was dead.

The World Mourns

For the next four days, Jacqueline Bouvier Kennedy "gave an example to the whole world of how to behave," in the words of French president Charles de Gaulle. In the face of horrific tragedy, she maintained supreme courage and dignity—and a sense of history.

Using President Abraham Lincoln's 1865 funeral as a model, Jackie planned Jack's funeral down to the last detail. The resulting ceremony was dignified, moving, and unforgettable. Millions of people around the world watched the grieving widow, holding her children's hands, stand before the **caisson** that would take Kennedy's casket to the Capitol, where his body would lie in state. They watched as she led the funeral procession from the Capitol to St. Matthew's Church for the funeral mass. In front of her walked a black riderless horse, symbolizing a fallen leader, with empty boots reversed in its backward stirrups. Beside and behind her marched the Kennedy family; the new president, Lyndon B. Johnson; and hundreds of world leaders.

Millions of people watched as she lit the eternal flame at John F. Kennedy's grave at Arlington National Cemetery. She wanted the whole world to remember—and they did.

Vietnam

The problem of Vietnam, left unsolved at Kennedy's death, haunted the United States for the next fourteen years. Like Kennedy, President Lyndon B. Johnson felt he could not abandon South Vietnam to communism. Gradually, he escalated the war. By 1967, 500,000 U.S. soldiers were fighting in Vietnam's jungles and villages. Yet, the United States still was not victorious. The war dragged on into the presidency of Richard Nixon, who vowed to bring the boys home. A cease-fire was declared in January 1973. Two years after the United States pulled out, North Vietnam overran South Vietnam.

In the end, no one won. More than 57,000 U.S. soldiers were killed, 300,000 were wounded, and 5,000 were missing in action. For Vietnam, the cost was even higher—a devastated countryside and 5 million casualties.

Would President Kennedy have plunged the nation into full-scale war, too? Some scholars say not. They say that he was already discouraged by the failures of South Vietnam's leadership and would have pulled out. Yet, we will never know.

John Jr. salutes his father at the funeral on November 25, 1963. John, who turned three that day, had loved playing soldiers with the president. As the casket was placed on the caisson, his mother leaned down and whispered to him, "John, you can salute Daddy now and say good-bye to him."

Who Killed Kennedy?

That tragic day in Dallas sparked decades of controversy over who was ultimately responsible for the Kennedy assassination. More than forty years later, many people are convinced that we still don't have the final answer.

Within hours of the assassination, police had apprehended the alleged killer—an unstable loner named Lee Harvey Oswald. A former Marine, he had been dishonorably discharged from the Corps before traveling to the Soviet Union and attempting to defect. When he was refused citizenship, he returned to the U.S. with his Russian wife and drifted from job to job. He ordered a high-powered sniper's rifle before Kennedy's visit to Dallas and took it with him to work at the Texas Book Depository the morning of the scheduled motorcade. As Kennedy's car drove by, Oswald took aim.

We will never know exactly why Oswald shot Kennedy because Oswald himself was killed just two days after his arrest. He was being moved from one jail to another when a Dallas nightclub owner, Jack Ruby, rushed through a crowd of reporters and shot him. The murder was captured live on national TV. Oswald died shortly thereafter. Ruby insisted that he killed Oswald to avenge Kennedy's death and spare Mrs. Kennedy a trial.

On November 29, 1963, President Johnson appointed a commission headed by Supreme Court Chief Justice Earl Warren to study the assassination. For nearly a year, the Warren Commission interviewed 552 witnesses, replayed tapes of the motorcade, and considered evidence. The commission decided that Oswald had acted alone.

This conclusion did not convince many people. The fact that Ruby had silenced Oswald before he was interrogated made them think that the Kennedy assassination was a conspiracy. Somebody didn't want Oswald to talk. Who could it be? There seemed to be many likely suspects. Perhaps responsibility lay with pro-Castro Cubans, who were angry with Kennedy because of the Bay of Pigs and the Cuban Missile Crisis. Maybe organized crime was to blame. President Kennedy's brother Robert was involved in an ongoing investigation of the Mafia, and Oswald and Ruby both had Mafia connections. Perhaps the CIA had wanted Kennedy dead because they opposed his foreign policy. Maybe guilt lay with homegrown **reactionaries** who hated Kennedy because he supported civil rights. It is worth noting, however, that Ruby himself always insisted that he was "innocent regarding any conspiracy."

Over the years, there have been many conspiracy theorists who have attempted to prove many conspiracy theories, but no one has offered convincing proof. In the end, we're left with what we know: an insignificant drifter trained a rifle on a president of the United States and changed the course of history.

Kennedy's assassin, Lee Harvey Oswald, shows off his rifle in March 1963, eight months before he used it to kill the president.

CHAPTER SEVEN

THE LEGEND

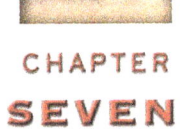

In the desolate weeks after the assassination, Jackie Kennedy was sustained by her children. "I have nothing else to do in life now except to raise my children well," she told Kennedy's press secretary, Pierre Salinger, "to help them move forward through this terrible thing—otherwise, they will be tied forever to their father's death. I have to make sure they survive." The day of Kennedy's funeral, she held John Jr.'s third birthday party in the White House nursery. From then on, the foremost mission of her life was to give Caroline and John Jr. a normal childhood.

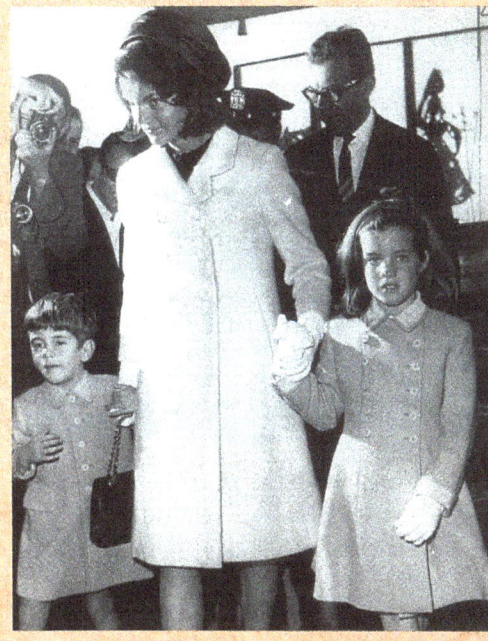

After her husband's death, Jackie devoted her life to caring for and protecting her children, John Jr. and Caroline, shown here on May 12, 1965. Wherever they went, they were the subject of obsessive press scrutiny.

She tried to settle down in Washington, D.C., but was dismayed when her town house became a tourist attraction. Far better, she thought, to move to New York City, where even the most famous can find a measure of privacy and anonymity. She bought a fifteen-room apartment on Fifth Avenue and filled it with antiques, old master drawings, Indian miniatures, and mementos from her life with Jack. It would be her home base for the rest of her life.

In January 1964, Jackie spoke on television to thank the world for its outpouring of sympathy. "I want to take this opportunity to express my appreciation for the hundreds of thousands of messages—nearly 800,000 in all—which my children and I have received over the past few weeks. The knowledge of the affection in which my husband was held by all of you has sustained me.... All his bright light is gone from the world."

At a party in Athens, Greece, to celebrate her fortieth birthday, Jackie walks with her husband of nine months, Aristotle Onassis (on right), August 1, 1969.

Jackie devoted herself to maintaining the Kennedy legacy. She and Bobby Kennedy, bound together in profound grief, became working partners in the design for the Arlington Cemetery site and the John F. Kennedy Library. She supported Bobby in his bid for the Senate, and then the presidency.

Jackie was devastated when, on June 6, 1968, Bobby Kennedy, too, was murdered while campaigning for the Democratic nomination. Her most immediate worry was for Caroline and John Jr. "I wanted to go away," she said later. "They were killing Kennedys, and I didn't want them to harm my children. . . . I wanted to be somewhere safe."

Where safer than a Greek island? Shipping magnate Aristotle Onassis, who owned his own island in the Mediterranean Sea, had been pressing Jackie to marry him for months. Bobby's death forced a decision. In October 1968, she wed Ari in a private ceremony in the presence of only her children and a few friends. Americans were shocked that the beautiful, still-young woman would marry the short, unattractive Onassis, twenty years her senior. A friend warned Jackie she was going to fall off her pedestal. "Better than freezing there," she replied. Besides, Onassis's enormous wealth would shelter her and her children.

An Independent Life

Onassis died a mere seven years later. Once again, Jackie was on her own. Even though she didn't need the money, she decided it was time to go to work. To the astonishment of her family and friends, she went back to her first love—books. For eighteen years, she worked in publishing, first at Viking and then at Doubleday, coming in three mornings a week and working on projects of her own choosing. Her books reflected her own passionate, eclectic tastes: Indian art, French history, architecture, art, and ballet.

The Kennedy Children

Famous from birth, Caroline Kennedy and John F. Kennedy, Jr., grew up under their mother's watchful eyes. Jackie was determined to protect them from the press and eager for them to explore their own interests. The general consensus is that the Kennedy children did grow up to be remarkably healthy, unspoiled, pleasant, and hard-working. "My mother parented for two," John Jr. said. "I'm glad people think it worked."

Caroline graduated from Harvard University and Columbia Law School. In 1986, she married Edwin Schlossberg, a cultural historian and museum designer. With a law school friend, she published two books, *In Our Defense—The Bill of Rights in Action* (1990) and *The Right to Privacy* (1995). She chose not to have a full-time career, however, preferring to devote most of her time to her family—Rose, born in 1988; Tatiana, born in 1990; and John, born in 1993.

She remained very close to her brother, John Jr. He chose to break with Kennedy tradition by earning his undergraduate degree at Brown University, then proceeding to New York University Law School. Trailed by the press when he failed the bar examination twice, he said philosophically, "I'm very disappointed. But . . . I'll go back there in July and I'll pass it then . . . or when I'm ninety-five." Of course, he did pass and worked in the Manhattan district attorney's office before quitting and founding a political magazine, *George*. His extraordinary good looks led *People* magazine to name him the "Sexiest Man Alive" in 1988. At age thirty-five, he married a publicist named Carolyn Bessette. His wife and her sister were with him on July 16, 1999, when his single-engine plane went down in the waters off Martha's Vineyard, Massachusetts. Their ashes were scattered in the sea not far from where they drowned. Caroline was left alone to mourn her brother and carry on the Kennedy legacy.

Jackie proudly walks with John Jr. after his graduation from Brown University in 1983.

Editing, Jackie felt, gave her an unparalleled opportunity to explore. "What I like about being an editor," she said, "is that it expands your knowledge and heightens your discrimination. Each book takes you down another path. . . ."

From left to right, Edward Kennedy; Jacqueline Kennedy Onassis; John F. Kennedy, Jr.; and Caroline Kennedy Schlossberg during a presentation of the JFK Profile in Courage Award in 1992.

She also used her influence to help preserve the city she loved. After joining New York's Municipal Arts Society in 1975, she fought to save landmark buildings from destruction. Thanks in large part to her intervention, Grand Central Station and other historic buildings were saved from the wrecker's ball.

Jackie always remained a celebrity. When she was sixty, her still-beautiful face graced the covers of *Life*, *Vogue*, and *Vanity Fair* magazines. Yet after thirty years in the public eye, she had finally carved out a satisfying personal life. Her constant companion for the last twelve years of her life was Maurice Tempelsman, a diamond merchant who shared her love of the arts. She treasured her three grandchildren, the children of Caroline and Caroline's husband, Edwin Schlossberg.

Then, her life was cut short at age sixty-four by non-Hodgkin's lymphoma, a cancer of the lymphatic system. On May 19, 1994, Jacqueline Bouvier Kennedy Onassis died in her Manhattan apartment, surrounded by family and friends and the books she loved so much. "She went out," Tempelsman said afterward, "with her usual courage and style."

Her former brother-in-law, Massachusetts senator Edward Kennedy, delivered her eulogy. "Jackie would have preferred to be just herself," Kennedy said at her funeral, "but the world insisted that she be a legend, too. She never wanted public notice—in part, I think, because it brought back painful memories of an unbearable sorrow, endured in the glare of a million lights."

TIME LINE

1917	John Fitzgerald (Jack) Kennedy born on May 29
1929	Jacqueline Bouvier born on July 28
1936	Jack enters Harvard University
1938	Joseph Kennedy appointed ambassador to Great Britain
1939	World War II begins
1940	Jack graduates from Harvard; *Why England Slept* is published; Jackie's parents divorce
1941	Pearl Harbor attacked December 7; U.S. enters World War II; Jack joins the Navy
1943	Jack saves crew of *PT-109*
1944	Joe Kennedy Jr. killed during WWII mission
1945	World War II ends
1947	Jack sworn in as congressman January 3; Jack diagnosed with Addison's disease; Jackie named "Debutante of the Year"; Jackie enters Vassar College
1948	Kathleen Kennedy killed in plane crash
1951	Jackie graduates from George Washington University and becomes a reporter at the *Washington Times-Herald*
1952	Jack elected senator from Massachusetts
1953	Jack marries Jackie on September 12
1956	*Profiles in Courage* published
1957	Caroline Bouvier Kennedy born on November 27; *Profiles in Courage* wins Pulitzer
1958	Jack wins second Senate race
1960	Jack wins the Democratic presidential primary on July 14; elected president on November 8; John Fitzgerald Kennedy, Jr., born on November 25
1961	Kennedy inaugurated January 20; Bay of Pigs invasion of Cuba, April 17; Alan Shepard completes suborbital flight, May 5; Berlin Wall built August 13
1962	Astronaut John Glenn orbits the Earth on Jan. 20; Cuban Missile Crisis takes place from Oct. 16–28; Jackie hosts TV tour of White House
1963	Kennedy civil rights bill to Congress, June 19; Nuclear Test Ban Treaty agreed upon, July 25; Patrick Kennedy dies August 9; March on Washington, August 28; Military coup in South Vietnam, November 2; John F. Kennedy assassinated, November 22
1968	Robert Kennedy assassinated on June 6; Jackie marries Aristotle Onassis on October 20
1973	Last U.S. troops withdrawn from Vietnam
1975	Aristotle Onassis dies; Jackie becomes becomes book editor
1994	Jacqueline Kennedy Onassis dies on May 19
1999	John Fitzgerald Kennedy, Jr.; Carolyn Bessette Kennedy; and her sister, Lauren Bessette, die in plane crash July 16

GLOSSARY

Bay of Pigs—small bay on the southern coast of western Cuba. It was the site of an ill-fated U.S. invasion on April 17, 1961.

blockade—blocking of a place, usually by ships, in order to prevent people or goods from moving in or out.

caisson—two-wheeled military vehicle drawn by a horse.

civil rights—rights belonging to an individual by virtue of citizenship.

Cold War—state of political tension and military rivalry that existed between the United States and Soviet Union following World War II.

communism—system of government in which one party holds power and property is owned by the government or community as a whole.

convoy—group, often of ships, that moves together for convenience or safety.

coup—violent overthrow of a government by a small group.

diplomacy—art or practice of conducting international relations, as in negotiating alliances, treaties, and agreements.

electoral college—group of people chosen from each state that gives the official vote for the president of the United States.

fascist dictatorship—system of government in which one person (most often) rules absolutely, and in which extreme nationalism, strict control of society and the economy, and suppression of all opposition is the norm.

House of Representatives—lower legislative house of the U.S. Congress.

inaugural address—speech given by a new president when he is sworn into office.

inauguration—ceremonial swearing in of a person into office, most often referring to a new United States president.

Joint Chiefs of Staff—principal military advisors to the president, composed of the chiefs of the Army, Navy, and Air Force and the commandant of the Marine Corps.

Korean War—conflict lasting from 1950 to 1953 between North Korea, supported by Communist China; and South Korea, aided by democratic United Nations forces, which mostly consisted of U.S. troops.

Kremlin—building which served as the seat of the central government of the Soviet Union.

legislation—act or process of enacting a law or group of laws.

Pearl Harbor—harbor west of Honolulu, Hawaii. It became the site of a naval base after the United States annexed Hawaii in 1900.

reactionaries—people who are extremely conservative in their political views and who do not support liberalism or change.

Reconstruction—period (1865–1877) after the Civil War when the Southern states were reorganized and accepted back into the Union.

segregation—policy or practice of separating people of different races, classes, or ethnic groups in society, especially as a form of discrimination.

Senate—upper house of the U.S. Congress, to which two members are elected from each state by popular vote and serve six-year terms.

Soviet Union, or Union of Soviet Socialist Republics (USSR)—former Communist country of Eastern Europe that included fifteen republics, including Russia. It officially ended on December 31, 1991.

suborbital—being or involving less than one orbit, as of the Earth or Moon.

totalitarian—relating to a government that controls all aspects of life, both social and economic, often by violent or suppressive means. The government is most often ruled by a dictator.

Vietnam War—long military conflict (1954–1975) between the communist forces of North Vietnam, supported by China and the Soviet Union; and the anti-communist forces of South Vietnam, supported by the United States.

FURTHER INFORMATION

Further Reading

Abraham, Philip. *John F. Kennedy and PT109*. (Survivor). New York: Children's Press, 2002.

Agins, Donna Brown. *Jacqueline Kennedy Onassis: Legendary First Lady.* (People to Know). Berkeley Heights, NJ: Enslow Publishers, 2004.

Cooper, Ilene. *Jack: The Early Years of John F. Kennedy*. New York: Dutton, 2003.

Coulter, Laurie. *When John and Caroline Lived in the White House: Picture Book.* New York: Hyperion Press, 2000.

Gormley, Beatrice. *First Ladies: Women Who Called the White House Home.* Madison, WI: Turtleback Books, 2004.

Gormley, Beatrice. *Jacqueline Kennedy Onassis: Friend of the Arts.* New York: Simon & Schuster, 2002.

Hampton, Wilborn. *Kennedy Assassinated! The World Mourns: A Reporter's Story.* New York: Candlewick Press, 1997.

Hargrove, Julia. *John F. Kennedy's Inaugural Address.* (History Speaks). Carthage, IL: Teaching and Learning Company, 2000.

Hawes, Esme. *The Life and Times of Jackie Onassis.* New York: Chelsea House, 1997.

Heiligman, Deborah, and Nancy Feresten. *High Hopes: A Photobiography of John F. Kennedy.* Washington, D.C.: National Geographic Society, 2003.

Kennedy, Caroline. *The Best-Loved Poems of Jacqueline Kennedy Onassis.* New York: Hyperion Press, 2001.

Kennedy, John F. *Profiles in Courage*. New York: HarperCollins, 2000.

Marcovitz, Hal. *John F. Kennedy.* (Childhood of the Presidents). Philadelphia: Mason Crest, 2002.

Mayo, Edith P. (ed.) *The Smithsonian Book of the First Ladies: Their Lives, Times, and Issues.* New York: Henry Holt/Smithsonian Institution, 1996.

Pietrusza, David. *John F. Kennedy.* (Mysterious Deaths). San Diego, CA: Lucent Books, 1997.

Santow, Daniel. *Jacqueline Bouvier Kennedy Onassis: 1929–1994.* (Encyclopedia of First Ladies). New York: Children's Press, 1998.

FURTHER INFORMATION

Places to Visit

John F. Kennedy Hyannis Museum
Hyannis, MA 02601
(508) 790-3077

John F. Kennedy Library
Columbia Point
Boston, MA 02125
(866) JFK-1960

John F. Kennedy Memorial Park
Maine, Commerce, and Market Streets
Dallas, TX 75202

John F. Kennedy National Historic Site
83 Beals Street
Brookline, MA 02446
(617) 566-7937

National Archives
700 Pennsylvania Avenue., N.W.
Washington, D.C. 20408
(866) 325-7208

The National First Ladies' Library
Education and Research Center
205 Market Avenue South
Canton, OH 44702
(330) 452-0876

Smithsonian National Museum of American History
14th Street and Constitution Ave. N.W.
Washington, D.C. 20013
(202) 633-1000

White House
1600 Pennsylvania Avenue, N.W.
Washington, D.C. 20500
(202) 456-2121

United States Capitol
Constitution Avenue
Washington, D.C. 20515
(202) 224-3121

Web Sites

AmericanPresident.org biography
www.americanpresident.org/history/johnfkennedy/

Jacqueline Kennedy timeline
www.fmnh.org/jkennedy/timeline.html

The John F. Kennedy Library
www.cs.umb.edu/jfklibrary/

John F. Kennedy timeline
www.worldhistory.com/jfk.htm

The National First Ladies' Library
www.firstladies.org

The Speeches of John F. Kennedy
www.jfklibrary.org/speeches.htm

The White House
www.whitehousekids.g

INDEX

Page numbers in **bold** represent photographs.

A

Addison's disease, 11, 18
Arlington National Cemetery, 37
Auchincloss, Hugh D., II, 14, 18

B

Bay of Pigs (Cuba), 27
Berlin Wall, 28, **32**
Billings, Lemoyne "Lem," **7**
Boston (Massachusetts), 10
Bouvier, Jack (Black Jack), **12**, 13
Bouvier, Jacqueline. *See* Onassis, Jacqueline Bouvier Kennedy (Jackie)
Bouvier, Janet, **12**, 13
Bundy, McGeorge, 28

C

Castro, Fidel, 27
Catholicism, 19
Central Intelligence Agency (CIA), 27
Chamberlain, Neville, 6
Chapin School (New York City), 13
Choate School (Connecticut), 7
civil rights, 21, 33, **34**
Cold war, 27, 30
communism, 27, 30, 34
Connally, John, **35**, 36
conspiracy theories, 38
coup, 34
Cuban Missile Crisis, **27**, 28-30

D

Dallas (Texas), 35, 38

E

Eisenhower, Dwight D., 19
electoral college, 21
Europe, 6, 7

F

Fitzgerald, John Francis (Honey Fitz), 5
France, 4, 6, 10

G

Gagarin, Yuri, 23
Germany, 6, 8
  division of, 28, 30
Glenn, John, **23**
Great Britain, 6
  declaration of war by, 8
  test ban treaty, 32

H

Harvard University (Massachusetts), 7
Hitler, Adolf, 6, 8
Horton, Ralph "Rip," **7**
Husted, John G. W., Jr., 15
Hyannis Port (Massachusetts), 17, **33**

I

inaugural address, 22, 26
Italy, 6

J

Japan, 9, 10
Johnson, Lyndon B., 20, **36**, 38
  Vietnam war, 37

K

Kennedy, Caroline Bouvier. *See* Schlossberg, Caroline Kennedy
Kennedy, Edward (Ted), **29**, 42
Kennedy, Eunice M., **5**, 11
Kennedy, Jackie. *See* Onassis, Jacqueline Bouvier Kennedy (Jackie)
Kennedy, John Fitzgerald (Jack), **4**, **22**
  assassination of, 36, 38
  birth and upbringing, 5, 6
  character traits, 7, 10
  charm of, 16
  congressman, as, 10, 11
  courtship and wedding, **16**, 17, **17**
  Democratic nomination, campaign for, 19, **19**, 20
  education of, 7
  faith, implications of, 19
  father, as, 25
  foreign affairs, interest in, 7, **8**
  funeral of, 36, 37
  health problems, 6, 8, 11
  heroism of, 10
  infidelity of, 18, 32
  leadership, style of, 20, 28
  military career, 8, 9, **9**, **10**
  popularity of, 23, 32
  president, as, 17, 22, **22**, 27, 28–30, 32, 34
  role model, as, 23
  style of, 24
  Vietnam, policy toward, 34
Kennedy, John Jr., 41
  birth of, 20, 25
  father, death of, **37**, 39
  death of, 41
  upbringing of, 25, **25**, **26**
Kennedy, Joseph Jr. (Joe), 5, 19
Kennedy, Joseph Patrick (father), **11**
  ambassador, as, 8
  businessman, as, 6
  Catholicism, implications of, 6
  family history, 5
Kennedy, Kathleen, **5**, 11
Kennedy, Patrick Bouvier, 32
Kennedy, Patrick J. (grandfather), 5
Kennedy, Robert Francis (Bobby), **11**, **29**, 38
  assassination of, 40
  Cuban Missile Crisis, 30
Kennedy, Rose Fitzgerald, 5, 7
Khrushchev, Nikita, 29, 30
King, Coretta Scott, 21
King, Martin Luther, Jr., 21, 33, **34**

M

March on Washington, 33, **34**
McCone, John, 30
McMahon, Patrick, 9
McNamara, Robert, 29
media, 21, 29, 39
Mussolini, Benito, 6

47

N

naval blockade, 30
New York City (New York), 39
Ngo Dinh Diem, 34
Nixon, Richard, 21
nuclear weapons, 28, 30, 32

O

Onassis, Aristotle, 40, **40**
Onassis, Jacqueline Bouvier
  birth of, 12
  Kennedy (Jackie), **4**
  baby, death of, 32
  character traits, 13, 36
  childhood of, 12, 13, 14
  children, devotion to, 39, 40, **41**
  death of, 42
  editor, as, 40
  family history, 12
  France, visit to, 4
  journalist, as, 15, **15**
  marital difficulties, 18, 32
  political campaigns,
    participation in, 20
  popularity of, 23
  privacy, need for, 25
  role model, as, 23
  second marriage of, 40
  teenager, as, 14
  wedding, **16,** 17, **18**
  White House, redecoration
    of, 24

organized crime, 38
Oswald, Lee Harvey, 38, **38**

P

Paris (France), 14
patriotism, 22
Peace Corps, 22
Pearl Harbor (Hawaii), 9
Poland, 8
Profiles in Courage (book,
  Kennedy), 19
Pulitzer Prize, 19

R

Rome-Berlin Axis, 6
Roosevelt, Franklin D., 8
Ruby, Jack, 38
Rusk, Dean, **28,** 30

S

Schlossberg, Caroline Kennedy,
  19, 41, **42**
  birth of, 19
  White House, life in, 25, **26**
Schlossberg, Edwin, 40
Shepard, Alan, 23
Soviet Union, 28, 30, 31
  test ban treaty, 32
  World War II, 10
space exploration, 23, **23**

T

Tempelsman, Maurice, 42
test ban treaty, 32

U

U.S.S.R. *See* Soviet Union

V

Vassar College (New York), 14
Vietnam, 34, 37
Vogue (magazine), 14

W

Warren Commission, 38
White House, 24
Why England Slept (book,
  Kennedy), 8
World War II, 10
  events leading to, 6
  Poland, invasion of, 8

About the Author

Ruth Ashby has written many award-winning biographies and nonfiction books for children, including *Herstory*, *The Elizabethan Age*, and *Pteranodon: The Life Story of a Pterosaur*. She lives on Long Island with her husband, daughter, and dog, Nubby.

www.ingramcontent.com/pod-product-compliance
Lightning Source LLC
Chambersburg PA
CBHW040855100426
42813CB00015B/2803